INSIGHT PUBLICA®

INSIGHT PUBLICA

Nadakkave, Kozhikode, Kerala, India
+91 4954020666 | +91 9400737475
www.insightpublica.com
e-mail: insightpublica@gmail.com
Cinderella
This Insight Edition: March 2020

ISBN 978-93-89155-29-7
Published by
Insightinpublica Publishers Pvt. Ltd.
Printed at Repro India Limited, India

Cinderella;
or,
The Little Glass Slipper and Other Stories

INSIGHT PUBLICA®

CONTENTS

CINDERELLA; OR THE LITTLE GLASS SLIPPER.

Once there was a gentleman who married for his second wife the proudest and most haughty woman that was ever seen. She had by a former husband two daughters of her own humor, who were, indeed, exactly like her in all things. He had likewise, by another wife, a young daughter, but of unparalleled goodness and sweetness of temper, which she took from her mother, who was the best creature in the world.

No sooner were the ceremonies of the wedding over but the mother-in-law began to show herself in her true colors. She could not bear the good qualities of this pretty girl, and the less because they made her own daughters appear the more odious. She employed her in meanest work of the house: she scoured the dishes, tables, etc., and scrubbed madam's chamber and those of misses, her daughters; she lay up in a sorry garret, upon a wretched straw bed, while her sisters lay in fine rooms, with floors all inlaid, upon beds of the very newest fashion, and where they had looking-glasses so large that they might see themselves at their full length from head to foot.

The poor girl bore all patiently and dared not tell her father, who would have rattled her off; for his wife governed him entirely. When she had done her work she used to go into the chimney-corner and sit down among cinders and ashes, which made her commonly be called a cinder maid; but the youngest, who was not so rude and uncivil as the eldest, called her Cinderella. However, Cinderella, notwithstanding her mean apparel, was a hundred times handsomer than her sisters, though they were always dressed very richly.

It happened that the King's son gave a ball and invited all persons, of fashion to it. Our young misses were also invited, for they cut a very grand figure among the quality. They were mightily delighted at this invitation, and wonderfully busy in choosing out such gowns, petticoats, and head-clothes as might become them. This was a new trouble to Cinderella, for it was she

who ironed her sisters' linen and plaited their ruffles. They talked all day long of nothing but how they should be dressed.

"For my part," said the eldest, "I will wear my red velvet suit with French trimming."

"And I," said the youngest, "shall have my usual petticoat; but then, to make amends for that, I will put on my gold-flowered manteau and my diamond stomacher, which is far from being the most ordinary one in the world."

They sent for the best tire-woman they could get to make up their head-dresses and adjust their double pinners, and they had their red brushes and patches from Mademoiselle de la Poche.

Cinderella was likewise called up to them to be consulted in all these matters, for she had excellent notions and advised them always for the best, nay, and offered her services to dress their heads, which they were very willing she should do. As she was doing this they said to her:

"Cinderella, would you not be glad to go to the ball?"

"Alas!" said she, "you only jeer me. It is not for such as I am to go thither."

"Thou art in the right of it," replied they. "It would make the people laugh to see a cinder wench at a ball."

Any one but Cinderella would have dressed their heads awry, but she was very good and dressed them perfectly well. They were almost two days without eating, so much they were transported with joy. They broke above a dozen of laces in trying to be laced up close, that they might have a fine, slender shape, and they were continually at their looking-glass. At last the happy day came. They went to Court, and Cinderella followed them with her eyes as long as she could, and when she had lost sight of them she fell a-crying.

Her Godmother, who saw her all in tears, asked her what was the matter.

"I wish I could—I wish I could—"

She was not able to speak the rest being interrupted by her tears and sobbing.

This Godmother of hers, who was a fairy, said to her: "Thou wishest thou

could'st go to the ball. Is it not so?"

"Y—es," cried Cinderella, with a great sigh.

"Well," said her Godmother, "be but a good girl, and I will contrive that thou shalt go." Then she took her into her chamber and said to her: "Run into the garden and bring me a pumpkin."

Cinderella went immediately to gather the finest she could get and brought it to her Godmother, not being able to imagine how this pumpkin could make her go to the ball. Her Godmother scooped out all the inside of it, having left nothing but the rind; which done, she struck it with her wand, and the pumpkin was instantly turned into a fine coach, gilded all over with gold.

She then went to look into her mousetrap, where she found six mice all alive, and ordered Cinderella to lift up a little the trapdoor, when, giving each mouse as it went out a little tap with her wand, the mouse was that moment turned into a fine horse, which altogether made a very fine set of six horses of a beautiful mouse-colored dapple-gray. Being at a loss for a coachman, Cinderella said:

"I will go and see if there is never a rat in the rattrap—we may make a coachman of him."

"Thou art in the right," replied her Godmother. "Go and look."

Cinderella brought the trap to her, and in it there were three huge rats. The fairy made choice of one of the three which had the largest beard, and having touched him with her wand he was turned into a fat, jolly coachman, who had the smartest whiskers eyes ever beheld. After that she said to her:

"Go again into the garden, and you will find six lizards behind the watering-pot. Bring them to me."

She had no sooner done so but her Godmother turned them into six footmen, who skipped up immediately behind the coach, with their liveries all bedaubed with gold and silver, and clung as close behind each other as if they had done nothing else their whole lives. The fairy then said to Cinderella:

"Well, you see here an equipage fit to go to the ball with. Are you not pleased with it?"

"Oh! yes," cried she; "but must I go thither as I am, in these dirty rags?"

Her Godmother only just touched her with her wand, and at the same instant her clothes were turned into cloth-of-gold and silver, all beset with jewels. Ah! who can describe a robe made by the fairies? It was white as snow, and as dazzling; round the hem hung a fringe of diamonds, sparkling like dewdrops in the sunshine. The lace about the throat and arms could only have been spun by fairy spiders. Surely it was a dream! Cinderella put her daintily gloved hand to her throat, and softly touched the pearls that encircled her neck.

"Come, child," said the Godmother, "or you will be late."

As Cinderella moved, the firelight shone upon her dainty shoes.

"They are of diamonds," she said.

"No," answered her Godmother, smiling; "they are better than that—they are of glass, made by the fairies. And now, child, go, and enjoy yourself to your heart's content."

But her Godmother, above all things, commanded her not to stay till after midnight, telling her at the same time that if she stayed one moment longer the coach would be a pumpkin again, her horses mice, her coachman a rat, her footmen lizards, and her clothes become just as they were before.

She promised her Godmother she would not fail of leaving the ball before midnight, and then away she drives, scarce able to contain herself for joy. The King's son, who was told that a great Princess, whom nobody knew, was come, ran out to receive her. He gave her his hand as she alighted out of the coach; and led her into the hall among all the company. There was immediately a profound silence, they left off dancing, and the violins ceased to play, so attentive was every one to contemplate the singular beauties of the unknown newcomer. Nothing was then heard but a confused noise of "Ha! how handsome she is! Ha! how handsome she is!"

The King himself, old as he was, could not help watching her and telling the Queen softly that it was a long time since he had seen so beautiful and lovely a creature.

All the ladies were busied in considering her clothes and headdress, that they might have some made next day after the same pattern, provided they

could meet with such fine materials and as able hands to make them.

The King's son conducted her to the most honorable seat and afterward took her out to dance with him. She danced so very gracefully that they all more and more admired her. A fine collation was served up, whereof the young Prince ate not a morsel, so intently was he busied in gazing on her.

She went and sat down by her sisters, showing them a thousand civilities, giving them part of the oranges and citrons which the Prince had presented her with, which very much surprised them, for they did not know her. While Cinderella was thus amusing her sisters, she heard the clock strike eleven and three-quarters, whereupon she immediately made a courtesy to the company and hastened away as fast as she could.

Being got home, she ran to seek out her Godmother, and after having thanked her she said she could not but heartily wish she might go next day to the ball, because the King's son had desired her.

As she was eagerly telling her Godmother what had passed at the ball her two sisters knocked at the door, which Cinderella ran and opened.

"How long you have stayed!" cried she, gaping, rubbing her eyes, and stretching herself as if she had been just waked out of her sleep. She had not, however, had any manner of inclination to sleep since they went from home.

"If thou hadst been at the ball," said one of her sisters, "thou would'st not have been tired with it. There came thither the finest Princess, the most beautiful ever was seen with mortal eyes. She showed us a thousand civilities and gave us oranges and citrons."

Cinderella seemed very indifferent in the matter. Indeed, she asked them the name of that Princess, but they told her they did not know it, and that the King's son was very uneasy on her account, and would give all the world to know who she was. At this Cinderella, smiling, replied:

"She must, then, be very beautiful indeed. How happy you have been! Could not I see her? Ah! dear Miss Charlotte, do lend me your yellow suit of clothes which you wear every day."

"Ay, to be sure," cried Miss Charlotte; "lend my clothes to such it dirty cinder maid as thou art! I should be a fool."

Cinderella expected well such answer and was very glad of the refusal, for she would have been sadly put to it if her sister had lent her what she asked for jestingly.

The next day the two sisters were at the ball, and so was Cinderella, but dressed more magnificently than before. The King's son was always by her, and never ceased his compliments and kind speeches to her, to whom all this was so far from being tiresome that she quite forgot what her Godmother had recommended to her, so that she at last counted the clock striking twelve when she took it to be no more than eleven. She then rose up and fled as nimble as a deer. The Prince followed, but could not overtake her. She left behind one of her glass slippers, which the Prince took up most carefully. She got home, but quite out of breath, and in her old clothes, having nothing left her of all her finery but one of the little slippers, fellow to that she dropped. The guards at the palace gate were asked if they had not seen a Princess go out.

They said they had seen nobody go out but a young girl, very meanly dressed, and who had more of the air of a poor country girl than a gentlewoman.

When the two sisters returned from the ball Cinderella asked them if they had been well diverted and if the beautiful Princess had been there.

They told her yes, but that she hurried away immediately when the clock struck twelve, and with so much haste that she dropped one of her little glass slippers, the prettiest in the world, which the King's son had taken up; that he had done nothing but look at her all the time at the ball, and that most certainly he was very much in love with the beautiful person who owned the glass slipper.

What they said was very true, for a few days after the King's son caused it to be proclaimed, by sound of trumpet, that he would marry her whose foot this slipper would just fit. They whom he employed began to try it upon the Princesses, then the Duchesses and all the Court, but in vain. It was brought to the two sisters, who did all they possibly could to thrust their feet into the slipper, but they could not effect it.

On the following morning there was a great noise of trumpets and drums, and a procession passed through the town, at the head of which rode the King's son. Behind him came a herald, bearing a velvet cushion, upon which rested a little glass slipper. The herald blew a blast upon the trumpet, and then read a proclamation saying that the King's son would wed any lady in the

land who could fit the slipper upon her foot, if she could produce another to match it.

Of course, the sisters tried to squeeze their feet into the slipper, but it was of no use—they were much too large. Then Cinderella shyly begged that she might try. How the sisters laughed with scorn when the Prince knelt to fit the slipper on the cinder maid's foot; but what was their surprise when it slipped on with the greatest ease, and the next moment Cinderella produced the other from her pocket! Once more she stood in the slippers, and once more the sisters saw before them the lovely Princess who was to be the Prince's bride. For at the touch of the magic shoes the little gray frock disappeared forever, and in place of it she wore the beautiful robe the fairy Godmother had given to her.

The sisters hung their heads with sorrow and vexation; but kind little Cinderella put her arms round their necks, kissed them, and forgave them for all their unkindness, so that they could not help but love her.

The Prince could not bear to part from his little love again, so he carried her back to the palace in his grand coach, and they were married that very day. Cinderella's stepsisters were present at the feast, but in the place of honor sat the fairy Godmother.

So the poor little cinder maid married the Prince, and in time they came to be King and Queen, and lived happily ever after.

FANNY'S TELEPHONE ORDER.

Little Fanny Desmond was a dear child, and, like a good many other little children, she liked to do whatever she saw the grown people do.

She would listen with great interest when she saw her mother use the telephone. She was especially surprised when her mother ordered things, and later in the day they would be brought to the house.

"I wish I had a telephone of my own," she said to her papa. "Mama just puts her mouth up to that funny thing, and gets whatever she asks for. Yesterday she asked somebody to send us ice-cream for dinner, and sure enough, it came."

Papa laughed. "It does seem a very convenient thing," he said. "I will try to arrange one for you." So papa took a horn which had been put away in a closet and hung it up where Fanny could talk into it. "There, that shall be your own private telephone," he said.

"Now, shall I get whatever I ask for?" said Fanny.

"Not if you ask for impossible things," replied her papa.

"But what are impossible things?" asked Fanny.

"Well," laughed papa, "I think if you should ask for the moon you would not get it."

"But I don't want the moon," said Fanny.

"Ask for something before I go down-town," said papa.

Fanny thought a moment, and then spoke up quite distinctly:

"Please send me some peppermints, and some new shoes for my doll, and a bunch of pansies for my mama, and a new bicycle for my papa, and—and—that's all this time. Good-bye."

"That's a very good order," said her papa, "but kiss me good-bye, for I must be off."

About half an hour later the front door-bell rang. Very soon the maid appeared with a package directed to Miss Fanny Desmond. In great excitement, Fanny opened it. It was a box of peppermints. The child's delight was great, but when, in another half hour, there came a bundle which proved to be a new pair of shoes for her doll, she was too happy for words. But that surprise was hardly over when another package was brought her. She opened it in great excitement, and behold there was a bunch of beautiful pansies.

"They are for you, mama," she cried, "and now everything has come but papa's new bicycle."

Just then she looked out of the window, and there was her papa coming up the drive on a fine new wheel. She rushed down to meet him, exclaiming, as she threw herself into his arms:

"Oh, papa, papa, I did get everything; my telephone is beautiful, and the man at the other end is just lovely!"

"Ah," said papa, "I am delighted he is so satisfactory."

THE RAINDROPS' NEW DRESSES.

"We're so tired of these gray dresses!"
Cried the little drops of rain,
As they came down helter-skelter
From the Nimbus cloud fast train.

And they bobbed against each other
In a spiteful sort of way,
Just like children when bad temper
Gets the upper hand some day.

Then the Sun peeped out a minute.
"Dears, be good and do not fight,
I have ordered you new dresses,
Dainty robes of purest white."

Ah! then all the tiny raindrops
Hummed a merry glad refrain,
And the old folks cried: "How pleasant
Is the music of the rain!"

Just at even, when the children
Had been safely tucked in bed,
There was such a rush and bustle
In the dark clouds overhead!

Then those raindrops hurried earthward,
At the North Wind's call, you know,
And the wee folks, in the morning,
Laughed to see the flakes of snow.

SIR GOBBLE.

Bessie Curtis was in a great deal of trouble. She was spending a year in the country while her father and mother were in Europe. It was not that which was troubling her. She liked the country, she loved her uncle and aunt with whom she lived, and she heard every week from her father and mother. But something disturbed her. As the summer passed, and the autumn came, she had moments when she looked very sober. What was the reason?

I will tell you.

Early in the spring her uncle had given her a young turkey.

"There, Bessie," he had said, "that is one of the prettiest turkeys I have ever seen. I will give him into your care, and on Thanksgiving Day we will have him on the dinner-table."

For some time Bessie fed the turkey every day without feeling particularly fond of him. Very soon, however, he began to know her; he not only ran to meet her when she brought him his corn and meal, but he would follow her about just the way Mary's little lamb followed HER about.

Her uncle often called after her: "And everywhere that Bessie goes, the turkey's sure to go."

Yes, round the garden, up and down the avenue, and even into the house itself the turkey followed Bessie.

Then why was she so sad?

Alas! she remembered her uncle's words when he gave her the turkey, "On

Thanksgiving Day we will have him on the table."

Thanksgiving Day would be here in a week.

Now, if Bessie had been like some little girls, she would have told her trouble to her uncle. But she never mentioned it to any one, although she cried herself to sleep several nights before Thanksgiving Day.

At last the day came, and Bessie, instead of going out to the fowlyard as usual, kept in the house all the morning. She was afraid that, if she went, she would not find her beloved friend. Dinner-time came, and, with a heavy heart, she seated herself at the table. Her uncle and aunt noticed her sober face, and thought that she missed her father and mother.

"Come, come," said her uncle, "we must cheer up; no sad looks on Thanksgiving Day. Maria, BRING IN THE TURKEY."

Poor Bessie! she could not look up as the door opened, and something was brought in on a big platter. But, as the platter was placed on the table, she saw that it did indeed hold her turkey, but he was alive and well.

She looked so astonished that suddenly her uncle understood all her past troubles.

"Why, Bessie," he said, "did you think I would kill your pet? No, indeed, but I told you he should be on the table Thanksgiving Day, so here he is."

Then Bessie's uncle struck the turkey gently with his carving-knife, the way the queen strikes a man with a sword when she makes him a knight.

"Behold!" said Bessie's uncle, "I dub you 'Sir Gobble;' you shall never be killed, but die a natural death, and never be parted from Bessie."

WHAT IS IT?

What is that ugly thing I see
Which follows, follows, follows me,
Which ever way I turn or go?
What is that thing? I want to know.

If I but turn to left or right
It does the same with all its might;
It looks so ugly and so black
When o'er my shoulder I look back.

Sometimes it runs ahead of me,
Sometimes quite short it seems to be,
And then again it's very tall;
I don't know what it is at all.

I'll climb into my little bed,
And on my pillow lay my bead,
For when I'm there I never see
That thing in front or back of me.

JOHN'S BRIGHT IDEA.

Mrs. Meredith was a most kind and thoughtful woman. She spent a great deal of time visiting the poor. One morning she told her children about a family which she had visited the day before. There was a man sick in bed, his wife who took care of him, and could not go out to work, and their little boy. The little boy—his name was Bernard—had interested her very much.

"I wish you could see him," she said to her own children, John, Harry, and Clara, "he is such a help to his mother. He wants very much to earn some money, but I don't see what he can do."

After their mother had left the room, the children sat thinking about little Bernard.

"I wish we could help him to earn money," said little Clara.

"So do I," said Harry.

For some moments John said nothing, but, suddenly, he sprang to his feet and cried:

"I have an idea!"

The other children also jumped up all attention. When John had an idea, it was sure to be a good one.

"I tell you what we can do," said John. "You know that big box of corn Uncle Sam sent us for popping? Well, we can pop it, and put it into paper bags, and Bernard can take it round to the houses and sell."

When Mrs. Meredith heard of John's idea, she, too, thought it a good one.

Very soon the children were busy popping the corn, while their mother went out to buy the paper bags. When she came back, she brought Bernard with her.

In a short time, he started out on his new business, and, much sooner than could be expected, returned with an empty basket.

Tucked into one of his mittens were ten nickels. He had never earned so much money before in his life. When he found that it was all to be his, he was so delighted he could hardly speak, but his bright smiling face spoke for him. After he had run home to take the money to his mother, John said:

"We have corn enough left to send Bernard out ever so many times. May we do it again?"

"Yes," said Mrs. Meredith, "you may send him every Saturday morning, if you will pop the corn for him yourselves. John, will you agree to take charge of the work?"

"Indeed I will," replied John, and he kept his word. For many weeks, every Saturday morning, no matter what plan was on foot, no matter how good the coasting or skating, he saw that the corn was all popped, the paper bags filled, and arranged in the basket when Bernard arrived.

People began to watch for the "little pop-corn boy," and every week he had at least fifty cents to take home, and often more. And all this was because of John's bright idea, and the way he carried it out.

A SAD THANKS GIVING PARTY.

Four hungry-looking animals
All seated in a row;
Why does not some one speak to them?
That's what I want to know.

They all of them were bidden to
A fine Thanksgiving feast,
And now, it seems to me, their host
Might welcome them, at least.

'Twas Master Pug invited them,
Why does he not appear?
'Tis plain they think his absence looks
Extremely rude and queer.

Alas! poor Pug's in trouble sore,
The host he cannot play;
No feast for self or friends has he
On this Thanksgiving Day.

He saw a turkey, large and fat,
Upon the kitchen shelf.
"That's just the very thing I want,"
Said he unto himself.

He caught the turkey, but the cook
Caught him with firmer grasp,
And shook him till he could not bark
But only choke and gasp.

Meanwhile, those hungry animals,
Who'd waited there in vain,
Declared they never would be guest
Of Mr. Pug again.

GUY AND THE BEE

One day a jolly bumble-bee,
In coat of black and yellow,
Got caught inside a window-pane;
The silly little fellow.

He buzzed and buzzed against the glass,
To Guy's great enjoyment,
Who thought to watch this funny thing
Was just the best employment.

But soon to touch those gauzy wings,
Became Guy's great desire,
Although mama had told him that
A bee could sting like fire.

But Guy, silly as the bee,
Paid no heed to mama,
He touched the bee, then gave a howl
Which could be heard afar.

Mama a soothing poultice mixed,
And on his finger laid.
"Another time you'll be more wise,"
Was everything she said.

A MEAN BOY.

Harry Burton woke one night and heard a strange noise in his closet. He got out of bed, crossed the floor in his bare feet, and carefully opened the closet door. The noise stopped, instantly.

"Ah!" said Harry, "I knew it was mice made that noise. How I wish I could catch them."

The next morning he told his mother about the noises he had heard.

"I will get you a mouse-trap," she said.

"I don't want the kind that kills the mice, I only want to catch them and tame them," said Harry.

His mother laughed and told him when he had tamed his mice he must keep them well out of her way.

The trap was set, the mice were caught, and sure enough, in a short time were so tame they would eat from Harry's hand. He made a little house for them, and kept in it his bedroom. Whenever he went out, he always shut the door carefully.

Now it happened that among Harry's acquaintances, there was one very disagreeable boy. His name was Dick Taft. Harry did not play with him very often, for he was so ugly it was hard to get along with him.

Dick never liked to be beaten at any game, and sometimes made it very uncomfortable for the one who got ahead of him.

One day Harry happened to beat him at one of their school games. Dick called after him when it was over, "I'll pay you for this, see if I don't."

Harry only laughed as he walked away going in the opposite direction from his own house.

When he was out of sight, Dick ran to Harry's house, made some excuse to go up in his bedroom, and let in the big cat, who was eagerly watching outside.

When Harry came home, the mouse house was open, and not one of his pets was to be seen. The poor fellow was almost heart-broken. He asked every one in the house who had left his door open. The maid told him she thought it must have been that boy he sent up to his room.

She described the boy, and Harry knew in a moment that it was Dick Taft.

"So that is the way he paid me for beating him at a game," cried Harry. "Well, never again, so long as I live, will I play with a boy who is mean enough to do such a trick as that."

And he kept his word.

A NAUGHTY PUMPKIN'S FATE.

A queer little pumpkin, a jolly fat fellow,
Stood close to his mother so rotund and yellow.
"What a stupid old place! how I long to aspire,"
Cried he, "I was destined for something much higher."

"My son," said the mother, "pray do be content,
There's great satisfaction in life that's well spent!"
But he shrugged up his shoulders, this pumpkin, 't is true,
And acted just like some bad children will do.

With a shout and a whoop, in the garden they ran,
Tom and Ned, for they'd thought of the loveliest plan
To astonish their friends from the city, you see,
With a fine Jack-o'-lantern—"Ah, this one suits me!"

Neddie seized the bad pumpkin, and dug out his brains,
Till he felt so light-headed and brimful of pains;
Then two eyes, a long nose, and a mouth big and wide,
They cut in a minute, and laid him aside

Until night, when they hung him upon a stout limb,
With a candle inside; how his poor head did swim,
As they twisted him this way, then twirled him round that,
Till at last, with a crash, he fell on the ground flat,

A wreck of the once jolly, fat little fellow,
Who stood by his mother so rotund and yellow.
Just then a lean cow, who was passing that way,
Ate him up, just to finish HER "Thanksgiving Day."

SOMETHING ABOUT FIRES.

It was a cold day. Fred was tired of reading, tired of looking out of the window, and so he poked the fire for a change.

"I suppose there are a good many different sorts of fires," he said to his mamma, as he laid down the poker.

"Yes, indeed," she answered. "It is very interesting to know how people keep warm in all parts of the world, especially where fuel is scarce and dear. In Iceland, for example, fires are often made of fish-bones! Think of that. In Holland and other countries a kind of turf called peat is dug up in great quantities and used for fuel. And in France a coarse yellow and brown sea-weed, which is found in Finistere, is carefully dried and piled up for winter use. A false log, resembling wood, but made of some composition which does not consume, is often used in that country. It absorbs and throws out the heat, and adds to the looks of the hearth and to the comfort of the room.

"The French have also a movable stove, which can be wheeled from room to room, or even carried up or down stairs while full of burning coke. In Russia the poorer people use a large porcelain stove, flat on top like a great table, with a small fire inside which gives out a gentle, summer-like warmth. It often serves as a bed for the whole family, who sleep on top of it.

"There are, besides gas-stoves, oil-stoves, various methods of obtaining warmth by heated air and steam, and, doubtless, other devices that I never heard of.

"In some countries, however, no fires are needed. In looking at pictures of tropical towns you will at once notice the absence of chimneys."

Fred looked admiringly at his mamma as she paused.

"There never was such a little mother," he said; "you can think of something to say about everything."

His mamma was pleased at this pleasant compliment.

"Oh!" she replied, laughing, "I could go on and tell you more about bonfires, beacon-fires, signals, drift-wood fires, and gypsy-tea fires; but I have told you enough for to-day."

THE ICE-KING'S REIGN.

The sun had gone down with promises sweet,
When, keen from the north, the wind
Came blustering along on its coursers fleet,
And left frozen tracks behind.

Maude stood at the window; the moon shimmered down
On whirling leaves, stiff and dead,
All piteously driven; she turned with a frown,
And soft to herself she said:—

"The old tyrant Winter leaves nothing to prize,
Leaves nothing that's bright or fair;
He has stolen the blue from the bending skies,
The warmth from the earth and air.

"The summer's dear blossoms are withered and dead;
My garden is brown and bare;
The chipper of birds in the nest overhead
Is hushed, for no birdlings are here.

"The woodlands no longer are shady and sweet,
Dry leafage encumbers the ground;
The pathways, once verdant and soft to my feet,
In fetters of ice are bound.

"The pride of the barn-yard sits humped with the cold,
One frozen foot under his wing;
And the sheep huddle closely, for warmth, in their fold;
The ice tyrant reigns as king."

She turns from this picture of ruin and death,
And seeks the broad casement again;

And, lo! from the dews of her wasted breath
Great forests have grown on the pane.

Such beautiful trees! such ferns! and such flowers!
Such rivers and mountains bold!
Such charming cascades! she gazes for hours,
And worships the ice king cold.

MALMO, THE WOUNDED RAT.

A poor man saw, by the roadside, a large white rat. It seemed to be dead. Moving it gently he found it was alive, but had a broken leg. He took it up and carried it to his lonely home. He bound up the bruised leg, fed the poor creature, and soon it was quite well.

Sam Tills trained the rat to gentle ways, and taught it many little tricks. Malmo was the only company Sam had. He worked in a cotton mill, and took Malmo with him. He rode in his master's coat-pocket. It looked droll to see his white head peeping out.

Sundays both went to dine with Sam's sister. Malmo's funny ways made everybody laugh. When Sam said, "Malmo, go sit in my hat," he went at once. He curled himself up in it, and nodded off to sleep.

When his master said, "Malmo, we're going now; slip in," the droll pet jumped from the hat, ran up to his pocket-nest, said good-by in his own fashion, and was ready to start. Evenings, when Sam was reading or singing from his mother's hymn-book, Malmo had a nap on his master's head. When it was time to go to bed Sam stroked Malmo's soft fur. The rat rubbed himself against his master's hand. It was their good-night to each other. Then Malmo crept into his basket, and the candle was blown out. Soon both were fast asleep.

MAMA'S HAPPY CHRISTMAS.

It had seemed to the little Wendell children that they would have a very sad Christmas. Mama had been very ill, and papa had been so anxious about mama that he could not think of anything else.

When Christmas Day came, however, mama was so much better that she could lie on the lounge. The children all brought their stockings into her room to open them.

"You children all seem as happy as if you had had your usual Christmas tree," said mama, as they sat around her.

"Why, I NEVER had such a happy Christmas before," said sweet little Agnes. "And it's just because you are well again."

"Now I think you must all run out for the rest of the day," said the nurse, "because your mama wants to see you all again this evening."

"I wish we could get up something expressly for mama's amusement," said Agnes, when they had gone into the nursery.

"How would you like to have some tableaux in here?" asked their French governess, Miss Marcelle.

"Oh, yes," they all cried, "it would be fun, mama loves tableaux."

So all day long they were busy arranging five tableaux for the evening. The tableaux were to be in the room which had folding-doors opening into Mrs. Wendell's sitting-room.

At the proper time Miss Marcelle stepped outside the folding-doors and made a pretty little speech. She said that some young ladies and a young gentleman had asked permission to show some tableaux to Mrs. Wendell if she

would like to see them. Mrs. Wendell replied that she would be charmed.

Then mademoiselle announced the tableaux; opening the doors wide for each one. This is a list of the tableaux: First, The Sleeping Beauty; second, Little Red Riding Hood third, The Fairy Queen; fourth, Old Mother Hubbard; fifth, The Lord High Admiral.

Miss Marcelle had arranged everything so nicely, and Celeste, the French maid, helped so much with the dressing, that the pictures all went off without a single mistake.

Mama was delighted. She said she must kiss those dear young ladies, and that delightful young man who had given her such a charming surprise.

So all the children came in rosy and smiling.

"Why, didn't you know us?" asked the little Lord Admiral.

"I know this," said mama, "I am like Agnes. I NEVER had such a happy Christmas before."

CURED OF CARELESSNESS.

Mrs. Bertram sat reading a book one morning, or trying to. It was not easy to do so, for her little boy, Roger, was out in the hall playing with his drum. Suddenly the drumming ceased, and in a moment Roger rushed into the room crying as if his heart would break.

"I've burst it. I've burst it," he sobbed.

"Your drum," asked his mother. "How did you do that?"

"I was beating it with the poker and the tongs and—"

"With the poker and tongs!" exclaimed his mother. "Why, where were your drum-sticks?"

Then Roger stopped crying, and hung his head with shame.

"Where are your drum-sticks?" asked his mother, again.

"I—I—don't know," sobbed Roger.

"Have you lost those, too?" said Mrs. Bertram. She needed no words for answer. Roger's manner was quite enough. "You know, dear, what I said would happen the next time you lost anything."

"Yes," said Roger, "I you said I must give away all my toys to some little boys who would take care of them."

"Yes," said his mother. "I see you remember. I shall send them all to-night to the Children's Hospital."

"But, mama," said Roger, "if I don't have any toys to take care of, how can I learn to take care of them?"

Mrs. Bertram had to turn away so that Roger should not see her smile.

"I shall have to think of some other way to teach you to be careful. Now go and bring me all your toys."

Roger went out of the room to do as his mother said. When he had gone, Mrs. Bertram sat thinking until he came back.

"I have decided that I want you to dust the library every morning."

Roger looked astonished. "Boys don't dust," he said.

"Sometimes," said his mother, smilingly. "Your Uncle Fred had to dust his own room when he was at West Point. Now if you dust the library every morning for two months faithfully, and do not break a single ornament, I shall know you have grown careful in one way, and that may help you to be careful in another."

The next morning Roger began his work. At first he disliked it very much, but after a while he grew very particular. It was not pleasant to be without any toys, and he determined to earn them.

The day when his trial of two months would be up, would be Christmas Day. He did not know if his presents this year would be toys or useful things. All his mother had said about his work was, "My dear, you are improving."

Christmas night came, and with it a beautiful tree. Imagine Roger's delight when he saw on and about it new skates, a new sled, a new violin and a new drum.

And up in the highest branches, in letters of gold, these words: "For the boy who has proved he can be careful when he tries."

A VISIT FROM A PRINCE.

Harry was playing with his letter blocks one afternoon, when a prince came to visit him.

Harry knew the prince very well, indeed. As soon as the prince came into the room Harry said:

"Hullo, old fellow, is that you?"

Was not that a very strange way to greet a prince?

And wasn't it stranger yet for Harry to say next:

"Come, sit up, old boy, and give us your—"

Was it hand Harry was going to say? No, indeed, it was paw. "Sit up, old boy, and give us your paw."

Prince was a beautiful dog, as black as a coal. Indeed, his real name, his whole name, was Edward, the Black Prince. Now you must ask somebody to tell you about the man who was called the "Black Prince," the man for whom Harry's dog was named.

When Harry asked Prince to give his paw, the dog did not do it as quickly as he ought to have done.

Did Harry beat him for that? No, indeed. Did he say, "Never mind, Prince, you need not obey me if you do not want to?" No, indeed, again.

He sat up himself, and then he made Prince sit up on his hind legs. Then he ordered Prince to give his paw. Prince did so. Then Harry made him do it again, then again and again and again, until the dog seemed to understand that he must learn to obey when he was spoken to.

After Prince appeared to have learned that lesson quite perfectly, Harry taught him something new.

He taught him to stand on his hind legs and hold a pipe in his mouth.

This he soon did so well that Harry clapped his hands and cried, "Good, good, you smoke as well as his royal highness, the Black Prince, himself."

Which remark showed that Harry had not yet begun to study history. If he had, he would have known that in the country where the Black Prince lived, tobacco was never heard of until many, many, MANY years after his death.

STRINGING CRANBERRIES.

Arthur Bancroft was feeling very cross one morning in December. He had a bad cold, and his mother did not think it would be wise for him to go out-of-doors. That was why he was cross. The skating was finer than it had been that season; every other boy he knew was enjoying it.

He walked about the house with a very sulky face; would take no notice of books or games, and seemed determined to be miserable.

He was standing looking out of the window when his sister Laura came into the room. Laura carried in her hand a basket filled with cranberries.

She put the basket on the table, took a needle from her mother's needle book, threaded it with a long, stout thread, and began stringing the berries.

Laura was a dear little thing! She was always busy. No one ever heard her say, "I wish I had something to do." And she was generally doing something for some one else.

She made a sweet little picture as she sat bending over the basket of crimson cranberries. Some such idea may have come into Arthur's mind as he turned and looked at her. As he watched her silently for some moments, the cross expression on his face became a little less cross.

"What are you doing?" he asked.

"Stringing cranberries for the Mullins' Christmas tree," answered Laura. "Don't you want to help me?"

"It's girls' work," replied Arthur.

"Isn't a boy smart enough to do a girl's work?" asked Laura.

"Of course, he's SMART enough. I don't mean that! Perhaps he doesn't want to."

"Oh," said Laura, "I wish you did want to."

"Why?" asked Arthur.

"I promised to string all these for the Mullins' Christmas tree," replied Laura. "The market-man brought them so late, I have not much time now."

"Thread another needle," said Arthur.

In a few moments he was working as busily as Laura, herself. As Arthur finished his last long string, he tied the ends together and threw it around Laura's neck. When she bent her head a little, it reached the floor.

"There," said he, "that proves that a boy can do a girl's work."

"Yes," said Laura, "when"—then she stopped and smiled.

"When what?" asked Arthur.

"When he has a girl to show him how," laughed Laura, as she danced out of the room with the cranberry strings.

CHRISTMAS IN CALIFORNIA.

"To think that this is Christmas Day!"
Said Harold to his aunt,
"I know it really is, and yet,
Believe it—well, I can't!
I've had a tree, my stocking, too,
This morning full I found,
But how can I believe it
With no snow upon the ground?

Look at the sea so bright and blue,
And feel the soft, warm air,
And there are roses all in bloom,
And lilies, I declare!
I think that California
Is lovely, but it's queer,
How different Christmas is at home
From what it is out here."

"Ah, Harold!" gently said his aunt,
"No matter where you go,
In country strewn with flowers like this,
Or clad in ice and snow,
The birthday of the Christ-child is
The same in every place,
And happy greetings in His name,
Bring smiles to every face."

A TROUBLESOME CALL.

We were going, on Saturday, ever so far,—
My mamma and I,—to the Dollies' Bazaar,
Where fifty wax dollies,—the loveliest show,
Went walking about when they wound 'em, you know.

You wouldn't believe half the things they could do:
Why, one said "Good morning," as plainly as you.
One played the piano, and one, dressed in lace,
Walked up to a mirror and powdered her face.

Well, when we were ready we stepped in the hall,
And there was a lady a-coming to call.
She said she just chanced to be passing that way,
And she really had only a minute to stay.

We waited and waited, and hoped she would go,
Till I saw it was almost the time for the show,
For I heard the clocks striking all over the town,
And I knew that the dollies would all be run down.

And so I just said, "I should s'pose, Mrs. Black,
Your little girl wonders why don't you come back."
That's all that I spoke, every 'dentical word;
But she said, "Little girls should be seen and not heard."

I guess that's a proverb, so maybe 'tis true;
But, if people won't see, what can little girls do?
My mamma looked queer, but that ended the call,
And we went to the Dollies' Bazaar, after all.

BERTIE'S CORN-POPPER

Bertie had the desire of his heart,—a corn-popper! He had wanted it for a long time,—three weeks, at least. Mamma brought it when she came home from the city, and gave it to him for his very own. A bushel of corn, ready popped, would not have been half so good. There was all the delight of popping in store for the long winter evenings.

Bertie could hardly wait to eat his supper before he tried his corn-popper. It proved to be a very good one. He popped corn that evening, and the next, and the next. He fed all the family, gave some to all his playmates, and carried a bag of pop-corn to school for his teacher.

Trip, the shaggy, little, yellow dog, came in for a share, and Mintie too. Who or what was Mintie?

Mintie was a bantam biddy, very small, white as snow, and very pretty. She had been left an orphan chick, and for a while kept in the house, near the kitchen fire. She had been Bertie's especial charge, and he fed and tended her faithfully.

As she grew older she would rove about with the larger hens, but was very tame, and always liked the house. She would come in very often. When Bertie happened to pop corn in the daytime she was pretty apt to be around, and pick up the kernels he threw to her.

One night he left his corn-popper on the kitchen table. It was open, and two or three small kernels were still in it.

Early next morning, long before Bertie was dressed, Mintie came into the kitchen. She flew up on the table, and helped herself to the corn in the popper. The girl was busy getting breakfast, and did not mind much about her. Presently she went down cellar, and Mintie had the room to herself.

When Bertie came down to breakfast there was a white egg in the corn-popper! It was so small that it looked almost like a bird's; but it was Mintie's first egg.

Bertie clapped his hands; he was very much pleased.

"Mamma! mamma!" he shouted. "See this pretty egg! Mintie put it into my popper, and must have meant to give it to me."

And mamma said, "Very likely she did."

FIRE! FIRE!! FIRE!!!

Where is it? Where is it? Why, it is in the water! Isn't that funny? But you see it isn't a real fire, but only a fire-fish. [*] Sweet creature, isn't he? Suppose you were a little, innocent mermaid, swimming alone for the first time; how would you feel if you were to meet this fellow darting towards you with his great red mouth open? Why, you would scream with fright, and swim to your mother as fast as you could, and catch hold of her tail for protection. At least, that is what I should do if I were a mermaid. But Mrs. Mermaid won't tell you that the fire-fish will not hurt you unless you hurt him first, in which case he will prick you dreadfully with his long, sharp spines.

I never see his picture without thinking of a red Indian in his warpaint and feathers. Perhaps—who knows?-perhaps when Indians are greedy, and eat too much fish, they may turn into fire-fish, and have to swim about forever under water, and never see a green forest again. If you are an Indian I advise you to be careful, my dear.

Nobody knows why this fish has such enormous, wing-like fins. Wise men used to think that he could raise himself out of the water with them, like the flying-fish; but it is now proved that he cannot, and there seems to be no reason why a set of plain, small fins would not serve him just as well for swimming. He prefers warm water to cold; so he lives in the tropical seas, swimming about the coasts of India, Africa, and Australia. The natives of Ceylon call him Gini-maha, and they think he is very good to eat. They take great care in catching him, for they are very much afraid of him, thinking that his sharp spines are poisoned, and can inflict a deadly wound. But in this they are too hard upon the fellow. He can prick them deeply and painfully, and he will if they meddle with him; but he is a perfectly respectable fish, and would not think of such a cowardly thing as poisoning anybody.

THE DOLLS AND THE OTHER DOLLS.

"Mamma," little Nellie asked, "is it right to give away things that have been given to you?"

Her mamma replied that it might be quite right sometimes; and she said, "But I should feel sorry if I had made a little friend a present she did not value, and so was glad to part with it."

"O mamma!" said Nellie, "you know how I value my dollies, every one, that my dear aunts and cousins sent me because I was sick. Now I am well again. To-morrow is New-Year's. Some sick little girls in the hospital want dollies. Could I, if I knew which one to choose, keep only one for myself, and send the whole five of them for those poor children who haven't any?"

Her mamma liked the plan. She gave Nellie a box, and Nellie began kissing her babies, and laying them, one after another, in the box.

There were two of nearly the same size, that were very dear to this little mother. She called them twins. They wore white frocks and blue kid boots. They had real blonde hair and their eyes would open and shut.

These lovely twins Nellie held in her arms a long time before she could decide which to part with. When she did place one in the box, to be her own no more, a tear was on the doll's cheek. I do not think the drop came from dolly's eye.

A few days after the dolls were given Nellie's mamma let her invite three little girls to play with her. Each girl brought her Christmas or her New-Year's doll; and the three dolls, with Nellie's, looked sweetly sitting together in a row.

By and by Nellie's mamma came to her room, which she had given to the party for its use that afternoon. She told the children she would give them a little supper of cakes and pears and grapes, and it would be ready as soon as Biddy could bring the ice-cream from down street.

The smiling child-visitors gathered around the kind lady, saying, "We thank you, and we love you ever so much."

Nellie said softly, "Mamma dear, I wouldn't take my dollies back if I could. I love to think they amuse the sick children. But I do wish that for just a minute we had as many at this party."

Her mamma turned to her dressing-case. It stood low enough for the smallest child to look into the mirror at the back easily. Moving off the toilet cushions and cologne-bottles, the lady put the four dolls in front of the looking-glass. Their reflection in the glass showed four more.

"Six, seven, eight," cried the girls, delighted. "And all are twins—four pairs of twins!"

After supper they made, the twins sit, and stand, and dance, bow and shake hands, before the looking-glass. So they played till dusk, when the other little girls' mammas sent to take them home, after kissing Nellie good-night.

WHY DID MAMMA CHANGE HER MIND?

Mamma Miller told Fay and Lonnie that they might have a party, so they tried to get ready for it. But the party was very different to what they expected. It always happens so about everything, if we pay no regard to one another's wishes.

Mrs. Miller said they might invite ten children.

"You write to five little girls, Fay," said she, "and Lonnie will write to the five little boys."

So they went into the library. Lonnie sat down in papa's big chair, while Fay climbed up on one arm, close beside him, and they tried to think whom they would like to come to their party.

"Make out your list first," said Lonnie. Fay did, and her brother agreed to all the girls. But as soon as Lonnie commenced writing his names, Fay began to find fault.

"I don't like boys, anyway," said Fay, "only you, Lonnie. Let's have all girls at our party."

"But it won't be my party," said Lonnie, "if you have all girls."

"I don't care, all those are horrid," pointing to his paper.

"You say that because you don't like boys." And then he told his sister that every little fellow whose name he had written was just as good as gold. And so they were just as good as Lonnie Miller, and he was one of the best boys that ever lived, so everybody said.

"I sha'n't play with him if he comes," Fay kept saying to every name Lonnie wrote.

"You can have your party," said Lonnie, getting up out of the easy-chair and sitting down in a smaller one, "you and your girls. I'm going to learn some new pieces," taking up his little silver blower.

"I don't like boys," Fay kept saying, jumping down off the arm of the chair, and aiming a blow at the spot where her brother had sat with the rustic stick their sister Lucia had brought home May Day.

Lucia was passing the door just then, so she thought she would see what all the noise was about.

"I'd better call you to lunch," said she, and there they were just through breakfast.

Mamma herself came hurrying in at sound of the bell. When they told her about the invitations, she said, "I shall not let you have any party at all, now."

"What makes you change your mind?" said Fay.

"Mamma will give her little girl just one week to find out why she has changed her mind," said Mrs. Miller.

And for all Fay's coaxing, she could not be persuaded to stay a minute longer.

CLARA'S "FUNERAL."

Clara was the most unfortunate of dollies. She had had the mumps and whooping cough; and no sooner did she recover from the scarlet fever than she contracted pneumonia and nearly died. One morning Blanche was applying hot bandages to relieve bronchitis, and before night Clara had the small-pox.

The next day mamma stopped at the nursery door.

"Good morning, little nurse," she said; "how is poor Clara this morning?"

"She's DEADED," said Blanche, with a long face.

"Dreadful! What did she die of, small-pox? It seems to me that that was what she was suffering from last evening."

"No'm'" said Blanche, "'twasn't small-pox. She DID have that bad; but I think she DIED of measles. The SUNERAL (Blanche could not say 'funeral') is to be at twelve sharp. Will you come, mamma?"

"I'm so sorry, darling, but I must go to lunch with Mrs. Mathews at one. But Jack will go."

The "suneral" took place at noon, and Blanche and Daisy, Jack and old Hector followed poor Clara in Benny's wagon to the grave yard at the bottom of the orchard. It was rather a jolly "suneral," for they had "refreshments" under the trees afterward.

In the afternoon, as mamma, came up the orchard path, she was surprised to see a doll's foot and leg sticking straight up out of the ground.

“Why did you leave her foot out in this way?” asked mamma.

“Well,” said Blanche, “I thought perhaps she could get to Heaven easier.”

THE CHICKADEE-DEE.

Little darling of the snow,
Careless how the winds may blow,
Happy as a bird can be,
Singing, oh, so cheerily,
Chickadee-dee! Chickadee-dee!

When the skies are cold and gray,
When he trills his happiest lay,
Through the clouds he seems to see
Hidden things to you and me.
Chickadee-dee! chickadee-dee!

Very likely little birds
Have their thoughts too deep for word,
But we know, and all agree,
That the world would dreary be
Without birds, dear chickadee!

THE CHILDREN'S PARTY.

What a merry, merry rout!
See the wee ones dance about!
Dickie's leading off the ball;
There,—he almost had a fall.

Who's his partner in the whirls,
—Rosiest of all the girls?
But a doll—a DOLL you say;
Dancing in that sprightly way?

Well I never! Oh, see there,
See—just see those horses tear!
Meg and Madge will sure be thrown.
What a vicious looking roan!

Not a real live horse you say,
Prancing in that frightful way?
Well, I never! Toys to-day
Surely seem more "real" than "play."

BRAVE TOMASSO.

There were once two very beautiful cats named Tomasso and Lilia. It would be very hard indeed to say which was more beautiful than the other, Tomasso the husband, or Lilia his wife.

They were about the same size, although, perhaps, Tomasso was a little the stouter of the two. There could be no question that at times the expression of his face was decidedly more fierce than that of his gentle wife.

The fur of each of them was as white as the driven snow, and as soft, and fine, and glossy as the most perfect silk gloss.

Add to these natural charms the fact that they always kept themselves beautifully clean, and always wore round their necks cravats made of the richest satin ribbon, and I am sure you will agree with me in thinking that they were cats of very high degree.

Their neighbors considered them extremely proud and haughty. They never were known to play with any of the cats in their street. To be with each other was all they asked. Sometimes these neighbors took a great deal of pains to get a glimpse of Tomasso and Lilia as, paw in paw, they danced a minuet together.

Even the most grumpy grimalkin declared it was a beautiful sight. There was no doubt the young couple was very graceful and their manners were perfect. Then he said that cats brought up as Tomasso and his wife had always lived, OUGHT to be amiable and beautiful. He understood that a jar of Orange County cream was ordered for them every day. Then he muttered something which sounded very much as if he thought Tomasso would be not over courageous in a moment of danger. "Alone, white tail is all very fine," said he, "but mark my word, at a sudden fright it would turn into a white feather. I should pity his wife if she had no one but him to protect her."

Now it happened that that very afternoon Tomasso's courage was put to the test. As he and Lilia were taking a quiet walk, suddenly a huge dog rushed out at them. In an instant Tomasso placed himself across Lilia's trembling body. She had fallen to the ground in terror. The great dog made a jump at Tomasso, but was met with such a snarl, and then such a blow from a set of sharp claws that he ran away howling.

That night the news of Tomasso's bravery spread through the whole neighborhood. But he was very quiet and modest. His proud wife was much disturbed at a bad scratch Tomasso had received in the struggle. They both examined it carefully with the aid of a hand-glass.

"I hope it will not leave a scar," said Lilia, "but if it does it will only be a proof of the noble courage of my brave Tomasso."

TOMMY FROST SEES A BEAR.

Tommy Frost was making his first visit in the country. He was enjoying it very much. He liked to ramble about in the woods close by the house of his aunt, Mrs. Drew. Tommy had never even seen any birds before this, but pigeons and sparrows. That is, any birds out of cages. He had lived all his short life in the centre of a great city. He wanted very much to see a wild animal. He had heard Mr. Drew and some of his friends talking about "bear tracks" in the woods. Mr. Drew said they must go off some day and hunt for that bear.

Now Tommy had no idea what a bear was like. He wished very much that he might see one. Every day he said to himself, "If I could only find the one the big men were talking about I'd feel proud." One day as he was strolling about, he suddenly saw something moving in one of the trees. He stopped, and looked up excitedly, then he rushed for the house screaming at the top of his voice, "Aunt Maria! Aunt Maria! come quick, I've seen it, it's in the woods."

"What is in the woods?" asked Mrs. Drew.

"The bear!" cried Tommy.

"The bear?" repeated Mrs. Drew, hardly understanding.

Then she drew a long breath and turned very white as she stood a moment shielding her eyes from the sun, looking in the direction in which Tommy pointed. Then she ran back into the house, and came out in a moment, bringing with her a huge horn. It was a megaphone. She was trembling so she could scarcely lift it, but she managed to raise it to her mouth and call through it. "John! Murray! come! come this instant! The bear is in the woods back of the house."

In a few moments her husband and brother came running from the field where they were at work.

They stopped for no questions, but rushed into the house for their guns. But as they came out Mr. Drew asked, "Who saw it? When, where?"

"I did," said Tommy, not a bit frightened, but feeling very excited and proud. "I did, back there in a tree."

"In a tree?" cried Mrs. Drew's brother, stopping in his quick run for the woods.

"Yes," said Tommy, "it was a bear, but it looked,—it LOOKED just like my picture of a wiggle-tail."

"Oh," cried Mrs. Drew, as she sank on the door-step, "the child has seen a gray squirrel!"

MYSELF.

One little head so smooth and round,
With soft hair covered, golden or brown,
One little forehead smooth and white,
Two little eye-brows dark or light.
Two little eyes that we see through.
See us looking, now, at you?
Two little cheeks so plump and round,
Where the red rose of health is found.
Two little ears where sound comes in;
One little nose and mouth and chin.
Rows of little teeth all in white;
Ready for use when lunch is in sight.
One little tongue kind words to say—
Bright little smiles which round them play.
One little head where all are seen.
One little neck which stands between
Head and shoulders to hold them fast.
Now are we ready to find, at last,
One little body with arms and hands
Two legs and two feet on which it stands.

TWO STRANGE SIGHTS.

"Oh come into the dining-room!"
Cries Fred, "come, grandma, dear.
For something very strange indeed
Is going on in here!"
And sure enough, when grandma comes,
Perhaps at first with fright,
She stands quite still, astonished at
An unexpected sight.

For there upon the woollen rug,
A jug between her feet,
Sits Freddy's little sister Bess
Absorbed in pleasures sweet.
Her finger in the syrup now
Behold she slyly dips,
And carries it with great delight
To her own rosy lips.

"You little witch!" cries grandmama,
"You're like the naughty rat
I found within the cellar once,
Who on a barrel sat,
Filled with molasses, which he reached
By dipping in the hole
His great long tail from which he licked
The sweets he thus had stole.

"The rat was shot, but grandma's babe,
Well, till she's learned to know
Such tricks are wrong, why we of course

Must naught but patience show."
Then grandma took her little pet,
And washed her sticky face,
Then put that tempting syrup-jug
Up in a safer place.

A CAT'S INSTINCTS.

"Take that! and that! and that!" These words came from an angry little girl. She was leaning over a big gray puss which she was holding down with one hand, while with the other she struck him a sharp blow every time she said "THAT."

It is a wonder puss did not bite her, for he was so strong he could have done so. He was a very gentle cat. "Gentle?" I hear some one ask. Then why did he deserve such a whipping as the little girl was giving him?

That is a question we must try to have answered. For my part I do not believe he deserved it at all. Let us see what happened next. Just as the little girl struck the last blow her Aunt Margaret came into the room. Aunt Margaret stopped in the doorway, astonished.

"Why Flora," she said, as puss darted out of the room, "what are you beating Griffin for?"

"What do you think he was doing?" cried Flora, her cheeks still flushed with anger. "He was on the table just ready to spring at this beautiful bird in my new hat. If I had not come he would have torn it to pieces."

"But he knew no better," said Aunt Margaret, "it is perfectly natural for a cat to spring at a bird. Yes, and for him to kill it too, if he has not been trained to do otherwise."

"But it would have made me feel dreadfully to have this beautiful bird torn to bits. I really love it. Besides, it was killed long ago."

"Yes," said Aunt Margaret, "killed that you might wear it on a hat."

There was something in Aunt Margaret's voice which made Flora and the little girls who were visiting her stand very still and look up.

"You say," continued Aunt Margaret very gently, "you say you love your beautiful bird. That you would feel dreadfully if it were torn to bits. How do you think its bird-mother felt when it was torn from her nest, and she never saw it again?"

"Oh," said Flora, "I never thought of that before. I'm afraid,—I'm afraid I'm more to blame than the cat."

DINAH'S NEW YEAR'S PRESENT.

Dinah Morris is a colored girl. She lives in the South. By South we mean in the southern part of the United States.

Dinah is one of the most good-natured children that ever lived, but she is very, very lazy. There is nothing she likes, or used to like, so much as to curl up in some warm corner in the sun and do nothing.

Dinah's mother wished very much that her child should learn to read, but the lady who tried to teach her soon gave it up. "It is no use," she said, "Dinah will not learn. She is not a stupid child, but she is too lazy for anything."

It happened, soon after this, that a young man from Massachusetts came to the house where Dinah lived. He brought with him something no one else in the neighborhood had ever seen before—a pair of roller-skates.

When Dinah saw the young man going rapidly up and down the piazza on his skates she was so astonished she hardly knew what to think. She ran after him like a cat, her black eyes shining as they had never shone before.

One day the young man allowed her to try on the skates. The child was too happy for words. Of course she fell down, and sprawled about the floor, but did not mind at all.

"Look here, Dinah," said the young man, "I understand that my aunt has been trying to teach you to read."

Dinah answered that she certainly had.

"Why didn't you learn?" asked the young man. "You need not trouble to answer," said he, "it was just because you are too lazy. Now, if, on the first of

January, you can read, I tell you what I will do. I will send you as good a pair of roller-skates as I can buy in Boston."

How Dinah's eyes snapped. For a moment she said nothing, then exclaimed decidedly, "I'll have those skates, sure."

And she did. When she bent her mind on her work she could always do it well, no matter what it was.

The lady who had before this found her such a difficult child to teach, now had no trouble. If Dinah showed the least sign of her former laziness the word SKATES! was enough to make her bend her mind on her lesson instantly.

On New Year's morning she received a box marked in large printed letters:

> MISS DINAH MORRIS,
> Care of Mrs. Lawrence Delaney,
> NEW ORLEANS, LA.
>
> If she can read what is on the outside of
> this box she can have what is inside.

And as Dinah read every word plainly and quickly, of course she had for her very own the fine roller-skates the box held. And now sitting curled up in the sun, doing nothing, is not the thing she likes to do best.

NIGHT FLOWERS.

There are some flowers that never see the sun. One of the most curious is the "evening primrose." About six o'clock it suddenly bursts open, with a popping sound, and at six next morning closes.

If you watch that pretty flower, and listen, you can hear this strange performance.

This is why it does so. The little calyx holds the petals in such a way that the moment it turns back they are let loose. At once it bursts out into full flower, with this funny noise, like a pop-gun.

So the "night-blooming cereus" blossom in the night, only for an hour, giving out its sweet fragrance, and then dies. Just think of never seeing the sun at all!

In a far Eastern country there is a kind of jasmine called the "sorrowful tree." It droops as if sick in the daytime, and at night grows fresh and bright. It opens its lovely flowers with a very pleasant odor till morning, and then wilts and looks wretched again.

THE FIRST SNOW-STORM.

Away off on a warm sunny island, little Harry Hall was born. Flowers bloomed all the year round. The sun shone most of the time, although now and then there were thunder-showers.

Many wonderful plants grew wild, while on the shore shells and seaweed and queer little fishes were often to be found.

When Harry was six years old his parents took a journey to New York.

It seemed very odd to the little boy to live in a place where there were so many people, and such great houses. After a while the weather grew cold, and he had to wear thick woollen clothing. The house in which they lived was heated by a furnace; but one day they had a fire of logs on the hearth. Harry enjoyed it very much, and thought the bright blaze so pretty.

The sky was gray and cloudy one afternoon, and Harry had been standing by the window watching the street cars. Suddenly the air grew thick, and he could scarcely see the houses opposite. Something white and feathery fell slowly down and rested on the window ledge. Then it disappeared. But more and more of the little flakes came, until there was quite a ridge outside of the window.

Harry opened the sash gently, fearing it might fly away. He was surprised when he touched it to find it so cold. He took some up in his hand, but in a moment it was only a drop of water.

By that time the street and the men's hats and coats were quite white. Harry was puzzled to find a name for the beautiful white substance, so he ran to his mamma and asked her about it.

She told him it was snow, and because the air was so warm on the beautiful island where he was born they never had any.

The next morning he saw the little children of the neighborhood playing in it; but before noon the sun was so bright and warm the snow had all melted away.

When the second snow-storm came Harry's papa brought home a beautiful sleigh, and gave his little boy great pleasure by drawing him up and down the street.

Harry soon learned to go out by himself, and made many friends; especially of the little girls, as he was very generous with his sleigh.

But he has never forgotten his surprise when he saw the first snow-storm.

FRED'S STOLEN RIDE.

One day little Fred's mother, who had been sick a long time, told him she was going out with a friend to take a drive. Fred wanted to go, too, but his mother said there would not be room in the buggy. Fred felt very cross and unhappy, and sat down on the front steps, ready to cry as soon as he should see his mother go away.

A buggy came to the gate, and the gentleman who was driving went into the house. Fred ran out and climbed into the buggy to sit there until his mother came out.

In looking around he saw there was a wide space under the seat, in which a boy might hide. He crawled in, thinking he would take a ride, and his mother would not know it.

He waited a long time, but no one came, and at last he grew tired and fell asleep.

He was waked by feeling a big jolt, as a wheel of the buggy struck a stone; but he kept still. After what seemed to him a long time the buggy stopped and he heard some one taking the horse from the shafts. He waited until all was quiet, and then crawled out from his hiding-place.

He found it was almost dark, and everything about him was strange. He was very much frightened, but he jumped down and went to a farm-house close by. A woman he had never seen before came to the door. When he told her where he lived she said he was fifteen miles from home, and he found that he had taken his stolen ride in the buggy of a man who had called to see his father on business.

It was too late for Fred to go home that night, and he had to stay at the farmer's house until the next day. Then he was taken home, and I am very sure he never tried to steal another ride.

A VALENTINE PARTY.

The children had a valentine party, the very nicest party,—they all declared, that they had ever been to in their lives. All the cousins in the neighborhood—and there were a lot of them—were there.

What fun they had opening their valentines, which a "really" postman brought with his gray uniform and his whistle and his great leather pack.

"Dear me," he said, pretending to groan, as he handed the missives, "if you had a party every day here I think I should be completely worn out!" But his eyes twinkled merrily.

Such shouts and exclamations as the valentines were opened and read! And such fun looking at everybody else's. Here are two, Bessie's and Fred's:—

I'm for the boy
Who can stand on his head,
And who NEVER likes
To go to bed.
If there's more than one of them,—
I'm for FRED!

I bring a kiss
From far away;
It's travelled many
Miles to-day.

Take it, my dear,
And send one back
To your old, loving
Uncle Jack.

Don't you think that the children OUGHT to have had a good time if all received as dear little valentines as these?

THE VENTURESOME RAT.

He was a fine young rat and lived with his father and mother, and brothers and sisters in a farm-cellar.

Now this young rat was not of a very quiet disposition. In fact he was quite gay, and thought the life in the farm-cellar was very dull and stupid and longed to see more of the world.

He sat near his father and mother one day when they were entertaining a caller, a stranger who seemed to have travelled all over the world, and told in a very interesting manner of the many wonderful things he had seen. "Why," said the caller, "how you can be contented to live as you do I cannot imagine, and to bring up your children in such ignorance fills me with surprise. They would learn more in one night prowling through the big house to which this farm belongs than they will learn here for the rest of their lives."

After this caller had taken his leave, the young rat decided that he would venture forth himself. He would that very night visit the big house and see what was to be seen there. He pretended to cuddle down on his own bed, and go sound asleep. He was really watching his parents out of the corners of his wicked eyes, and as soon as they were sound asleep, off he started. He found his way to the house much more easily than he had expected; in short, almost before he could believe it, he was in a fine great pantry. A pantry whose shelves were covered with such good things to eat as he had never seen. Rich cake, pies, cookies, and cheese such as he had heard the caller describe. The first nibble fairly melted in his mouth.

After he had eaten his fill he began looking about the pantry for other means of amusement. Suddenly he saw a curious thing; it seemed to be a little house or hut made of wire. Inside the hut was a piece of cheese. "I really think I have eaten enough," said the young rat, "but if that cheese is so fine that it is kept in a house by itself it must be very fine indeed." With these words he crawled into the hole in the side of the hut and ate the cheese, but when, later,

he tried to get out he could not to save his life.

Hours and hours he remained there until the night passed, and the day came. Indeed he had fallen into a little nap when he was awakened by a loud cry. Some one was shouting, "we've caught the rascal at last, now we'll drown him."

The poor little fellow knew they were wrong; he could not be the rascal they meant, for this was the first time he had ever been in the house. At that moment a boy's voice was heard to say. "Let me see him. No, you shall not drown him. I will tame him if I can."

And so it came about that the young rat did see a good deal of the world, but how? THROUGH THE BARS OF A CAGE.

THE BEARS' FEAST.

A man had come to town with two tame bears. They were very clever bears, and could climb posts and trees, dance and turn summersets and do a great many other tricks besides.

One day the man was taken ill and had to stay in the house all day. He thought the bears were locked up in the barn. But the bears decided they would go for a walk by themselves. They managed to get away without being seen and started in the direction of the schoolhouse.

The children were at recess when they suddenly saw the bears. They were frightened and ran screaming into the school-house.

The bears were very tame and kind and wanted to make friends with the children, so they followed them.

The children jumped on the desks screaming and crying and the teachers were frightened too.

When the bears saw that they could not make friends or play they began quietly walking about the school-room.

Finally they came to the dressing-room where all the dinner-pails and baskets were hanging.

Smelling the food, they managed to knock some of the baskets down and then such a feast as they had!

They sat on their haunches and ate sandwiches and fruit and drank milk out of the bottles just as the children would do. When they had eaten enough they quietly left the school-house and trotted down the road toward home.

After the bears were gone the children became calm again and returned to their lessons.

The man and the bears disappeared the next day and were never seen again.

PATTY-SAYINGS.

"I've been reading Bible stories," Patty said, "and I believe That Adam's name MEANT 'Morning,' Because his wife was 'Eve.'"

BABIE'S CURLS.

Little Bessie Boothby
Had a little sister Sue:
And a baby brother,
Whom she thought the world of, too.

Only one thing troubled
These dear little girls;
'Though baby Tom was pretty,
He hadn't any curls.

They found a box of vaseline
And rubbed it on his head;
But even then no hair would grow:
It made his head quite red.

Bessie once was brushing
Dollie's golden hair,
When off it fell, alas! and left
Poor dollie's head quite bare.

Little Sue was frightened,
But to comfort, Bessie said,
"Susie dear, do listen,
'Tis just like babie's head.

"Let's put the wig on baby Tom,
And then he'll have some curls;
I would not even be surprised
If he looked just like us girls."

When Mamma saw her baby boy
With all this growth of hair,

She laughed until she nearly cried,
At the naughty little pair.

THE RED APPLES.

One windy day in March Kitty Miller was on her way to school, when she spied in a store window, a great pile of lovely red apples.

"Oh," she said, "how lovely! if Mamma could only have one!"

Kittie's mother was very poor. She had been a dress-maker ever since Mr. Miller died, and had worked so hard to earn a living for herself and Kitty that she had become sick. She was obliged to lie in bed all day, and when Kitty was away at school, the house was very lonesome to the invalid.

When Kitty reached the school that day her thoughts were full of her sick mother and the lovely apples.

She was usually a good scholar, but to-day she made so many blunders that the teacher looked at her in surprise. The little girl could only sit at her desk, with her book before her, and dream of those red apples. When school was dismissed, Kitty started slowly homeward. She had gone only a short distance when she saw a gentleman in front of her drop his purse. Running quickly forward she picked it up. It felt quite heavy in Kittie's little hand.

"There must be a good deal of money in it," thought Kitty. "How I wish I could keep it. Then I could buy Mamma a red apple and so many other things she needs."

But she knew this would not be right, so she hurried after the gentleman. Touching him on the arm, she said, "Please, Sir, you dropped your purse."

"Thank you, dear," said the gentleman taking the purse.

Then noticing how poorly dressed she was, he said, "Why did you not keep the purse, my child?"

"Because that would be stealing," replied Kitty. "But," she continued honestly, "before I thought I must give it back to you, I did wish I could keep it, for then I could buy Mamma a red apple."

The gentleman smiled kindly and said, "You are a good little girl to return my purse. I would like to give you a little present and then you can buy a red apple."

He handed her a silver dollar and then bade her good-by.

Kitty was so surprised that she started hastily for home, forgetting all about the red apples until she stood in front of the store.

The store-keeper happened to look out and saw the same little girl who stood looking so longingly in at his window in the morning. He quickly picked out the biggest, roundest, reddest apple he could find and taking it out to Kitty said, "Would you like this, my dear?"

She took the apple, looking so pleased and thanking him so prettily, that the good man thought of it for many a day. When Kitty reached home with her treasures she found her mother fast asleep. So she put the apple and silver piece on a plate where her mother could see them when she awoke.

When Mrs. Miller was told the wonderful story, she kissed her little daughter and said, "You see, dear, it always pays to be honest and truthful."

BUBBLES.

"Now, Tommie, what will you do while I write letters this morning?"

"Blow soap bubbles, Mamma, please," and Tommie jumped up and down, clapping his hands for pleasure.

"Well, run and get me your pipe and bowl and I will mix you some suds."

The soap-suds were soon ready, and Tommie took his favorite position on the broad window-sill with the bowl in his lap.

Mamma, writing in the next room, could hear the Oh's and squeals of delight, as the bubbles grew larger and rounder.

"Why is Tommie in all the bubbles?" asked the little boy at last.

"Because," said Mamma, "the bubbles are like a mirror, and when my little boy is near enough to look at them, he will be reflected in them, just the same as when he looks in Mamma's long mirror."

"But the mirror doesn't break like the bubbles," said Tommie. "Where do they go when they break, Mamma?"

"They evaporate, dear; that is a big word for my little boy. Spell it after Mamma and then perhaps you will remember. E-v-a-p-o-r-a-t-e evaporate."

"What does evaporate mean," asked Tommie bringing out the long word with a jerk.

"Do you remember, dear," answered Mamma, "that early in the morning when the grass is all wet with dew, my little boy cannot run in it without his rubbers? But before long it is all dry and then my little boy takes off his rubbers and does not get his feet wet. The sun and the air absorb or suck up the

water and carry it off to their homes. Now, the bubbles are made of a little water and a little air. The water is on the end of the pipe, and Tommie blows the air into the pipe, and the bubble grows big and round. When it breaks, the air sucks up the water, which was the outside of the bubble, and the air which was inside mixes with the air in the room."

"Now do you suppose you can tell Papa all about it, when he comes home to dinner?" asked Mamma.

"Of course I can," said Tommie, proudly. "Haven't you just told me all about it?"

A HORSE WHO WORE SNOW SHOES.

Mr. Brown had to go to his camp at Pine Tree Valley, which is in the midst of the mountains in California.

His men were cutting down the giant trees, and piling them in readiness for the Spring freshet, or floods of the river, when the snows melted. Then they would slide them down the mountain sides to the little villages below.

There was a great deal of snow on the mountains, and Mr. Brown knew it would be hard work climbing to the camp, but Lady Gray was strong, and used to it.

Lady Gray was Mr. Brown's pet horse, and carried him everywhere. She was always happy when her master was in the saddle.

But to-day the snow was very deep and soon Mr. Brown had to get off, throw away the saddle, and lead her. They had to stop very often, and lean against the trees and rocks for support, while they rested and regained their breath.

In places the snow was so deep and soft, that they sank above their knees. Late in the afternoon they reached the camp nearly exhausted, and it was several days before they were able to return.

The snow was still deep and Mr. Brown knew he must go back on snow-shoes, but he was afraid Lady Gray would have to be left behind.

Finally one of the men suggested making her some snow-shoes. They cut four round pieces of board, twelve inches across, and fastened them on with rope. Lady Gray seemed to understand what they were for and tried very hard to walk in them.

She was very awkward at first and could hardly stand up, but by practicing a little every day she was soon able to manage nicely.

So Mr. Brown and Lady Gray both returned on snow-shoes, and how every one did laugh when they saw them.

But Lady Gray never could have done it if she had not tried.

THE ANGRY BOBOLINK.

Pretty little bobolink
In your satin coat,
Trimmed with white across the neck
Black about the throat,
Why so angry do you seem?
Why so fierce your mien?
That you're scolding somebody
Plainly can be seen.

"Don't you know," says bobolink,
As he shakes his head,
That my nest is hidden in
This soft grassy bed?
Somebody has come too near,
And I wish to say
There is no admittance here
Pass the other way.

"If my gentle little wife
Sits so calm above,
It's because she knows I'll guard
This dear nest we love."
Fear not, pretty bobolink,
Sing your joyous song,
Never will I trouble you,
Sing, the whole day long.

HOW HIRAM SPENT HIS SHRIMP MONEY.

"I wish my mother had a ring like those the ladies wear at the hotel," said Hiram Green to himself one day. "There isn't one of those ladies as pretty as my mother; she ought to wear rings too."

Hiram was the son of a fisherman, but the fisherman had died when Hiram was a little boy. Hiram's mother took in sewing and fancy work to earn money to support herself and her son. He helped her what he could out of school hours, and in vacation. He had two uncles who wad taught him how to catch shrimps. With the money he earned by selling them he could buy things for his own use or pleasure. He had a bank almost full of what he called his "shrimp-money." He did not mean to count his money until the bank was full.

Now Hiram loved his mother more than anything else in the world. Whenever he dreamed of being rich some time, as boys often do, it was not for himself he wanted the money, but that his dear little mother might drive in a carriage, drawn by a pair of horses with clanking chains.

The sight of the flashing gems on the hands of some of the summer visitors at the fishing village in which he lived had added a new article to the list of beautiful things his mother was some day to own. He had heard that just one single diamond was sometimes worth five hundred dollars or more. This had discouraged him very much. But one day happening to pass a shop in the neighboring town he saw a number of rings displayed in the window. Diamond rings which flashed and sparkled, it seemed to him, just as those worn by the ladies in the hotels. He stopped fascinated, ana pressed his face against the glass eagerly to see if any prices were marked upon them. Imagine his surprise when he saw upon the largest one a tag marked $4.75. He looked again to see if he had not made a mistake. Perhaps it was $475.00. But no, he knew enough about figures to see that he was right the first time.

Home he went as fast as he could get there, and ran up into his bedroom. Then, for the first time since he had begun to save his "shrimp-money" he opened his bank and counted its contents. "Three dollars and twenty-two cents!" he cried, "almost enough. I was going to buy something for myself this time, but I'll have that ring before another week."

Hiram worked early and late for the next few days. He caught more shrimps than he had ever caught in the same length of time, and sold them readily.

"I think there must be something you are wanting, very much, my boy," said his mother.

"Yes, there is," replied Hiram.

At the end of the week he had the sum he desired. Hurrying to the shop where he had seen the ring, before going inside he gave one hasty, almost frightened look into the window. Could it be gone! No, there it was flashing and sparkling as before.

That evening, he placed it on his mother's finger. She looked at it in surprise. "It is yours, mother," he cried, proudly, "your very own, I bought it with my shrimp money. I was determined my mother should have a ring as handsome as those ladies wear."

"My dear boy," said his mother, while something as bright as the shining stone flashed in her eyes, "Not one of those ladies can value their rings as I shall value mine."

Years afterwards Hiram learned that what he had bought for a diamond was only a bit of glass.

"Did you know it then, mother?" he asked.

His mother nodded. "And you never told me."

"It was brighter to me than any real diamond," she said, "the brightness I saw flash in it was the unselfish love of my boy."

THE ANT'S HOUSE.

"What a curious picture that is at the head of this story." That is what I think I hear some of the "Little Ones" say. "What does it mean?" some one asks. It looks like a procession of ants. That is just what it is. A procession of ants all marching off to find a new home. Some one has destroyed their old one. Let us hope no one did it on purpose.

The ants are very busy and very nice little creatures. If their houses are stepped upon, or injured so as to be useless the ants immediately go to work to repair damages. They do not sit down and fuss about it first, but I have no doubt they let each other know what they think. And how do you suppose they do this? By touching each other with their tiny feelers.

After they have talked in this way, and decided what is to be done some of them take the eggs from the ruins and carry them to a safe place. Look carefully at the pictures, and you will see that almost every ant is carrying an egg. They know that if they lose the eggs all the young ants inside the eggs will be lost too.

While ants do not seem to have a very keen sense of hearing, their sense of smell is very strong. And where do you think it lies? In the same little feelers with which they talk to each other. The first ant's house seen in the round picture has been cut in two to show you how wonderfully these little creatures can build.

It was made by the ants that live in tropical countries. The house at the back of the picture has not been disturbed. Does it not look as if an architect had planned it? Ask some of the older people in your family to tell you something more about ants. There is much more of interest in regard to them than I have space to write you.

THE FOOLISH PUG.

A pompous pug once thought that he
A dashing swell would try to be,
And on his neighbors one and all,
Sat out to make a stylish call.

He wore a glass upon one eye,
And on his head a silk hat high;
A wide, stiff collar around his throat,
And last an English overcoat.

So fine and splendid was his air
The very birds stood still to stare,
As walking on his two hind feet
He sauntered boldly down the street.

But oh, alas! it comes to all
To learn that pride must have a fall,
And e'er the corner he had turned
Poor pug that bitter lesson learned.

A saucy maid with one great whack,
Brought down her broom upon his back,
And as he raised a frightened wail
Another soused him from her pail.

Poor pug! that night he sat and thought
Of all the trouble he had brought
Upon himself, because that he
A foolish dude had tried to be.

THE SILHOUETTE PARTY

"Children," said Grandpa, one afternoon, "I am going to build a bonfire this evening, to burn up this rubbish, so you may have a silhouette party."

"Why, what is a silhouette party?" asked Lucy, opening her eyes very wide.

"I know," said Ralph, "it is funny black pictures on something white."

"That's right," laughed Grandpa. "Now you fly round and write your friends and Grandma and I will get everything ready."

When the young people arrived at half past seven, they found a blazing fire, and in front of it was stretched a sheet between two large apple trees.

Quite a distance in front of the sheet were some seats, where Grandpa told some of the children to sit, while the others took part in the pictures.

He then disappeared with them in a tent close by where Grandma was waiting to dress them in their different costumes. Shouts of laughter came from the tent as the children put on their odd dresses; indeed there was so much fun that it took quite some time.

When all was ready Grandpa came out and addressing the children who were waiting said, "These are to be Mother Goose pictures, which you will all know. You must guess whom they represent and the one who guesses correctly the largest number will receive a prize."

He threw a large pine knot on the fire, which burned up brightly, and there the children saw a shadow on the sheet, a little bent figure with a broom over its shoulder.

"The old woman who swept the cob-webs out of the sky," cried some one.

Following this, came a figure with a long cloak and tall peaked hat, leading a dog.

"Old Mother Hubbard," guessed another.

Then came a boy and a girl carrying a pail.

"Jack and Jill," chorused the children.

After this a girl with a shepherd's crook.

"Little Bo-peep," again was guessed.

"Now," said Grandpa, "it is time the others had their turn at acting."

So the exchange being made, the pictures continued.

"Jack Horner," "Little Miss Muffet," "Old King Cole," and "Mary, who had a little lamb," followed in quick succession.

Then Grandpa announced that the pictures were over.

"As we cannot decide who has guessed the largest number of pictures," said he, "I will give you each a prize." And he passed them each a card.

It proved to be a picture of Ralph and Lucy cut from black paper and pasted on a white card.

"These," said Grandpa, "are silhouette pictures too. Will you always know what a silhouette picture is now?"

"Oh yes," said the children.

THE SNOW BIRDS.

It had snowed very hard. Ralph and Edward, who were visiting Grandma in the country, had to stay in the house all day.

When they went to bed it was still snowing, and every time they woke up during the night, they could hear the wind sighing and whistling around the house, and through he branches of the old pine tres.

But the next morning the sun was shining brightly. Such a glorious day! How the branches of the pine trees did sparkle.

"It looks as if they had been sprinkled with gold dust and diamonds," exclaimed Ralph.

"Oh Grandma! Please do hurry breakfast. We are going out to build a fort," cried the boys, bursting into the dining-room.

Grandma smiled and told them to eat a good breakfast, for building a fort was hard work.

They were soon out in the snow, and what a splendid time they did have.

The fort did not grow very fast, for they had to stop so often to snow-ball each other.

When Grandma called them in to dinner they wondered where the time had gone since breakfast.

After dinner, Ralph was looking out of the window, when he spied two little birds cuddled up on a branch of a pine-tree.

"Oh, Edward! come here," he called. "See those poor little birds. They look half frozen and so hungry."

"Poor little things," replied Edward. "Doesn't it make you feel mean to think what a jolly time we had this morning out of the snow which has covered up the places where they get their food?"

"Let us get some food from Grandma and throw it out to them," said Ralph. "Perhaps they will find it."

The little birds were soon chirpping and flying about merrily and Ralph said it sounded as if they kept saying, "thank you."

Will not other little children be as kind as Ralph and Edward?

A KIND HEART.

The day Ethel Brown was seven years old she had a tea party.

Mrs. Brown had sent tiny cards of invitation to all the little girls on the street to come and bring their dolls. She also sent one to Nellie Day, her washer-woman's little girl, at Ethel's special request.

"She is a nice little girl," said Ethel, "and doesn't ever go anywhere like me. May I have her at my party?"

"That is right, little daughter," said Mrs. Brown. "Always be kind to those who have less pleasure than yourself. Of course she may come to your party."

They all arrived at four o'clock and looked very pretty in their white dresses and bright ribbons, and the dolls looked nearly as pretty as the little girls themselves.

Ethel noticed that Nellie Day did not have a doll with her. "So," thought she, "I will ask her to pour the tea and then she won't feel bad because she hasn't one."

The little girls talked and played games and Ethel's grown up sister played on the piano and then they sang.

"Now," said Mrs. Brown, coming into the room, "if you will choose partners, Florence will play for you and you can march out to tea."

During the confusion Ethel said to her mamma, "I shall ask Nellie to pour the tea because she has not any doll."

"Very well, dear," answered Mrs. Brown.

But when they turned to find her, she was not with the others.

"Where can she be?" exclaimed Ethel.

And then began the search. Tea was delayed and they hunted the house over for her. Finally Mrs. Brown went out on a side porch seldom used, and there she found the little girl.

The child had brought a cushion to sit on, and clasped tightly in her arms were three of Ethel's dolls. Mrs. Brown persuaded her to come in with the promise that she might keep the dolls.

So Ethel rang the bell, and they all marched in to tea again, with Nellie Day leading the line, holding her three dollies.

"Mamma," said Ethel, as the little girls were going home, "may I give Nellie Day the dolls? I have so many and she has not one."

"Yes indeed," replied Mrs. Brown, as she kissed her little daughter. "I am sure it will make her very happy."

And Nellie Day went home that night, the happiest little girl in the town.

TOWSER TALKS.

I am not a big dog and I don't know very much, but I know more than I used to. The reason why I know more than I used to is because I asked Carlo some questions once. I asked him what made him so gaunt and thin and why he had such an enquiring expression on his face and such a hump on the top of his head. He didn't answer right away, and—I noticed the enquiring expression vanished. He looked quite decided. Then something happened,—I don't know exactly what, but Mary, the cook, told the butler that it made her dizzy just to look on. And then Carlo said:—

"One reason why I am gaunt and thin is because I am not a little up-start of a pug,—of no earthly use under Heaven, and nothing to do but waddle around and accumulate fat.

"The reason I have an enquiring expression on my face is because I am ever on the outlook to anticipate my master's will and do his slightest bidding.

"As for the hump on the top of my head, that is a mark given by the Creator only to dogs that have intellect. Pray that yours may grow!"

That is all he said, but it was enough for one day and has furnished me food for thought ever since.

JUST AS SHE PLEASED.

"Now, children, I am tired of you; I am going down stairs for the rest of the morning," and Polly started to leave the nursery.

"Put your dolls away before you go," said Nurse, "I don't want them left in the middle of the floor."

"I won't. I did not put them there." Polly tossed her head and ran quickly out of the room.

Nurse had baby in her lap and could not run after her.

The little girl went to the kitchen, but cook was cross and said she would not have Polly bothering her.

Then she went to the library hoping to find her Uncle Edward, but he was not there.

She wandered from room to room and could find nothing to amuse her.

She wanted to go back into the nursery, but she had told a lie when she said she had not put the dolls on the floor, and she was afraid to.

She felt lonesome and a few tears ran down her face.

At that moment Uncle Edward entered the room, and, seeing the doleful little face, took her in his arms, tossing her into the air.

As he did so, he knocked over a vase which fell to the floor, broken.

"Oh! see what you have done," cried Polly.

"I don't care. I shall say I didn't do it," replied Uncle Edward.

"Oh! But that would be a lie," said Polly.

"Well, who put the dolls on the nursery floor?"

"Nurse must have told you. But I am sorry," and Polly began to cry again.

"There, there!" said Uncle Edward. "We will go up and tell Nurse we are sorry."

They went up to the nursery but Nurse and baby had gone and the dolls were still on the floor.

Polly wanted to play circus and Uncle Edward made believe he was the elephant and gave the dollies a ride. He kicked so once that black Diana fell off and broke her neck.

After a while Nurse came in with baby and interrupted the frolic.

When Polly told her she was sorry because she had told a lie, Nursie said she would forgive her and Polly promised not to do so again.

THE WORKING TOOLS OF INSECTS.

I wonder if you know that the smallest insects you see about you have tools given them to do their work with. There is a little fly called a saw-fly, because it has a saw to work with. It is really a very much nicer saw than you could make, if you were ever so old.

The fly uses it to make places where the eggs will be safe. What is more strange, it has a sort of homemade glue which fastens them where they are laid.

Some insects have cutting instruments that work just as your scissors do. The poppy-bee is one of them, whose work is wonderful. This bee has a boring tool, too. Its nest is usually made in old wood. This borer cleans out the nest ready for use. When all is ready the insect cuts out pieces of leaves to line the nest and to make the cells. These linings are out in the shape of the cells. You, would be surprised to see the care taken to have every piece of just the right size, so that it will fit. When they are fitted, the pieces are nicely fastened together and put into the nest.